The Backyard Play Revolution

How to Engage Kids in Simple,
Inexpensive Outdoor Play and
Increase Child Health and
Motor/Sensory Development

Jason Runkel Sperling

First Edition, 2016
http://www.JasonRunkelSperling.com

ISBN: 978-0692616468

To my children, Nyla and Silas. You inspire me with your inventiveness, every time.

Contents

Introduction...................................... **9**

Book Overview 12

A Call for Change **14**

Child Health and Development 24

The Backyard Play Revolution..........................27

Fundamentals **30**

Indoor vs. Outdoor Play......................................31

Convergent vs. Divergent Play........................... 33

Adult-Led vs. Child-Led Play..............................35

Loose Parts...35

Junk Playground.. 42

Backyard Playspace Opportunity 47

Risk.. 50

Playwork and Being a Playworker 58

Practice **67**

#1 Stick..67

#2 Rope 74

#3 Tire 84

#4 Bucket 90

#5 Sheet 95

#6 Water 99

7 Mud Kitchen 104

Ingredients 109

Organic...111

Junk/Recycled/Hardware 112

Textile... 114

Kitchen 114

Farm Supplies & Equipment 115

Landscaping Materials 116

Construction Materials 117

Reflections 118

The End.. 119

Extra Help To Get Started 119

About the Author............................120

Other Books By Jason......................122

The print version of *The Backyard Play Revolution* does not include links to research and resources cited throughout the text that appear as hyperlinks in the digital version.

For these links, please visit:
http://www.jasonrunkelsperling.com/
revolutionlinks

Introduction

Having two children and observing hundreds of others, it is clear that the sphere of influence as a parent is limited. Children enter the world with their own personalities and potential. Yet we have a vital role in the nurturing of our children through the food, environment, education, and social and cultural experiences we provide as parents. But the times they are a-changin'. In just the past couple of generations—and for the first time in human history—toys have become a major influence in raising children. Children now spend more time indoors than outdoors, and children's ability to partake in unstructured play has all but vanished.

From the birth of my daughter and for the last six years (during which time my young son was born), I've meticulously tested, observed, and refined the experiences I provide for my children (now ages three and six). Like any new parent, my hope was to evolve from an Aspiring Good Dad to a Super Dad, so I was eager to find ways to not only capture my children's attention, but also contribute to their physical, emotional, mental, and social development. As costs of supporting a family continued to spiral beyond my wildest anticipation (I mean, seriously?!), my evaluation of toys and experiences also centered on return on investment. I don't want to spend money on toys that turn out to be garbage and break hours after purchase, or find hundreds of toys building up in my house and gathering dust because there's just too much. I don't want to enroll my children in activities to prep as an Olympian that they'll never be or get scholastically ahead when academic education isn't what they need. I don't want to make them play in ways and places to satisfy my adult goals. I want what is best for them.

I'll admit that I wasn't exactly following pure scientific method in my experimentation. But as I watched and tried new things, I began to notice patterns. A hypothesis began to form in my exhausted mind, but with only two children—and being time starved—I eventually turned to research to accelerate my understanding and validate my suspicions. I researched obsessively, night after night, month after month—buying dozens of books and poring over the Internet, devouring every article and piece of educational material I could find. I talked to my children's teachers, to friends, to my own parents.

What I discovered about the history of child-raising, play, and parenting styles around the globe profoundly affected my view and day-to-day approach in raising my own children. I've discovered that:

- The dominant culture of mass-produced and marketed toys is new.

- Young children's capabilities are far-reaching, and we are overprotecting them.

- Play, and especially risky play, is vital to children's growth.

- There isn't good guidance for parents in how to best participate in children's play.

- Questioning the status quo is confronting and challenging, but critical.

- The setup in our homes greatly determines children's play opportunities and outcomes.

The results of this curiosity—of this quest—have given me much delight. I am confident in the choices I make for my children. More importantly, I've witnessed repeatedly the joy and happiness with which my children find their play when it is unstructured, outdoors, and with the right materials.

This book presents the results of these six years of experimentation and research.

Warning

What I have learned and share in this book may seem counterintuitive. The findings challenge the beliefs of the majority. My own belief system and faith in common practices have been shaken, and this can be terribly inconvenient. Friends and relatives have often found themselves at the opposite end of a spectrum from me when it comes to children's toys and children's play. Ironically, the "toys" I've found to be the best— the ones that blow other toys away in price, replay, and longevity—consist of tried and true tools for child development. The toys that seem to perform the best have much of human history backing their success, and they directly impact how the children play.

Book Overview

In this book, I share my discovery, practices, and ingredients for successful backyard play. I believe this is a tremendous value for children age two to six. This book has been inspired by my personal journey, verified by decades of research, and championed by children around the world.

In the first part of the book, I share what I've learned as I've delved into the world of Loose Parts, Adventure Playgrounds, Risky Play, and Playwork.

In the second part of the book, I provide seven different accounts of my experiences in the backyard, examples of how to do it yourself in practice, and where you can get the materials.

My hope is that you can read the entire book today and take action tomorrow. Nothing has proved more rewarding to me than finding ways to help my children in their own journeys.

A Call for Change

Being a parent is challenging. From sleep deprivation to an almost total eclipse of personal free time and disposable income, raising children is not for the weak of heart. My own challenges are no doubt the result of a personal fault: I have found that being with my children inside the house is so acutely painful that I rarely want to do it. Remove their highchair restraints and put them on the floor and they explode from neutral to fifth gear, bombing around the house like cartoon Tasmanian Devils, whirling, damaging property, a wild mess flanking out behind them like an ocean liner's wake, the walls echoing with their cacophony of screams and wails....

On the other hand, give children electronics and they become zombies, glued to the screens with such ferocity that taking the device away causes a storm of emotions to rival a category five hurricane. And if you attempt to explain the constraints of time and space—"Don't run into the wall," "It's time for dinner"—children transform into monsters, a species of their own making. This isn't particularly surprising, since inside spaces are designed for adults. Indoors are meticulously optimized for adult operation, enjoyment, and entertainment. Put any wild animal into a cage and watch them do the same as young children...bounce off the walls.

To avoid this special kind of madness—certainly one that I regard as a personal failure—I found myself evicting the children—and myself—out to the backyard at every possible moment. And it was in the backyard where I humbly witnessed the demons gracefully exit my children. Bewilderingly amazed, I watched them bloom with imagination and a pleasantness that has made me love being a parent. Of course, it didn't last. Not immediately, anyway.

Our backyard began like most. On the weekends we spent time manicuring it, planting new things, and dreaming of how we might landscape the grounds to create our ideal outdoor experience. There was a swing set and sandbox for the children, as well as a good-sized lawn with apple, maple, aspen, and poplar trees scattered about. We were working at making the space one that met our adult preferences.

Then it happened: the Geodesic Dome Day.

My daughter, Nyla, got a geodesic dome for her fourth birthday. As I labored, assembling the dozens of pieces and hundreds of bolts, I could barely contain my excitement. I fondly remembered the geodesic dome at a park from my childhood and was thrilled that my daughter was going to have one of her own—her very own!—that she could use whenever she wanted. I figured she would live on this thing. Live! I would herd us out from the living room into the long-stretching vistas of the backyard and there upon the geodesic dome she would play. The monster would be sedated and I would have a chance to breathe and unwind.

Hours later, the assembly complete, I invited Nyla to test the dome. I was so excited. She was so excited. She shrieked, she climbed, she hung. So much fun.

Nyla excitedly awaiting construction of the geodesic dome.

After that day, the geodesic dome wasn't used all that much. She didn't live on it. Weeks would go by where she wouldn't even go near it. Like it was diseased. Every couple of days I had to remember to rotate and slide it a few inches to avoid the grass getting yellowed and decayed where the pipes rested on the ground, tainting my precisely manicured backyard. Each time I moved it, I resented how much it had cost, how it blighted my backyard, and, most importantly, how little Nyla was using it. How could this be? The pictures in the marketing materials, on the website, and in the videos were of children having so much fun. They were jubilant. Gleeful. Was something wrong with my daughter? Or me?

To this day, the geodesic dome remains an expensive and rarely used toy.

The geodesic dome is not alone. The bulk of toys we have, indoor and outdoor, are rarely used. I don't mean to bash all toys or the type of play they facilitate. My daughter loves to put on skits with dress-up clothes. She'll play Uno with me (cheating unabashedly) until we're both starved from fasting on the couch with a sparse diet of lukewarm water and seedless grapes. My son loves driving his fleet of cars and trains around with such gusto that we now need to refinish our wood floor—Silas 1, Floor 0. Magnetic tiles and Legos are a huge hit too. I love those as much as the kids, and have often daydreamed of making my profession be one where I play, as an adult, with building toys for toddlers. And give the children crayons or an iPhone loaded with apps and they can disappear for an entire airplane ride.

But I'm talking about real value here—toys that get epochs of playtime. Good play that enriches their development. Toys and play that stir their imaginations and provoke beautiful social interactions. The kind of moments you want to take videos and photos of, post to Instagram and Facebook instantly, and treasure forever.

The disaster of the geodesic dome thrust me into research. With good fortune, I stumbled upon the surprising and wondrous world of Loose Parts, Adventure Playgrounds, and Playwork. While there's much ado in parenting about picking the right school, feeding the right food, and disciplining and nurturing the right morals in children, I had to go looking for this world. It feels subterranean. Loose Parts doesn't even have an entry on Wikipedia. Playwork isn't in the majority of parenting books and magazines or talked about at play dates. Loose Parts, Adventure Playgrounds, Playwork, and my resulting experiments fly in the face of mainstream marketing of play and toys. They challenge the idea of how to optimally present unique educational and developmental opportunities for children. And Loose Parts are available at a price that fairly democratizes children's toys.

Loose Parts are open-ended materials that children can manipulate on their own, are interoperable, and by definition have no fixed purpose. These can range from organic materials like stones and dirt to construction materials like lumber and rope, and even include textiles like sheets and pillows. They are simple, inexpensive, and often not thought of as toys. Yet give a child a cardboard box and see his imagination skyrocket far beyond that of the package's contents. Loose Parts are highly effective toys for play, learning, and child development. Yet there remains little information, instruction, or resources for parents to easily fill their backyards with Loose Parts. It is not possible, for example, to go to Amazon and buy the deluxe Loose Parts set. This is a shame, because, from my experience, Loose Parts are the cheapest, best, fastest way to engage children in your backyard in a profound way. While I go into more detail about Loose Parts shortly, once I discovered their incredible value, I wondered why there isn't more readily available information.

From the research that I've studied and that I share in this book, there are a number of factors that are influencing the limited visibility of Loose Parts. To begin with, we have companies that began to target children as a niche market in the 20th century.

Thunder Burp Machine Gun—Fully Automatic Cap Gun

Prior to 1955, advertising at toy companies was minimal and only allowed companies to promote toys on television during the Christmas season.

"But then came Mattel and the Thunder Burp, which, according to Howard Chudacoff, a cultural historian at Brown University, was a kind of historical watershed. Almost overnight, children's play became focused, as never before, on *things*—the toys themselves" (The Evolution of Play, NPR, 2008). This changed toys forever, making play an industry and children a demographic—a target market that companies began investing in heavily.

Companies are profit-focused, so their goals are to increase the purchases of toys using sophisticated tactics that make toys extremely appealing and addictive (versus being crafted for learning, even though the toys are frequently marketed to support early child development).

Where did "go outside and play" go?

The environment for parenting has also changed dramatically. There is an increase in dual-working parent families and single parent families, and an increase in the emphasis on making sure children prepare for the future or "get ahead," all reducing the quantity of unstructured free play time.

"Children's free play and discretionary time declined more than seven hours a week from 1981 to 1997 and an additional two hours from 1997 to 2003, totaling nine hours less a week of time over a 25-year period in which children can choose to participate in unstructured activities" (Childhood Development and Access to Nature, Hofferth and Sandberg, 2001; Hofferth and Curtin, 2006).

Educational institutions and other structured programs foster the belief that learning requires adult-led activities, and devalue child-led playing. While there are exceptions, there is little evidence that children need more than what generations (centuries, in fact) of children have used as their tool to learn: play. Meanwhile, homes have increased in size, while publicly available land for play has decreased. Parents' fear of allowing children to roam independently at early ages has led to a decline in the use of the outdoors as a learning and play environment. The concept of "go out and play" has, for the most part, gone out with the bathwater.

As I learned about Loose Parts, I discovered Adventure Playgrounds (seemingly the birthplace of Loose Parts from an academic perspective). Adventure Playgrounds are a specific type of playground with equipment, materials, objects, and an environment that children can manipulate and interact with through child-led activities. Adventure Playgrounds around the world put American playgrounds to shame. They also present opportunities for risky play that stunned me: children leaping off high heights, playing with fire, and interacting with waterways in spellbinding ways. As I learned about risky play and its importance in child development, I became acquainted with convergent and divergent play (convergent play, where a child solves a problem with a single solution, versus divergent play, where a child solves a problem with many solutions), open-ended toys, and Playwork (a formalized theory and practice of creating and maintaining spaces for children to play). I realized the folly of the geodesic dome, and the ineptitude of the majority of toys available to children.

Delving into the history of childhood, I discovered mind-blowing accounts of children's capabilities at early ages, such as the long-held traditions of children in indigenous cultures when it comes to handling their own knives and spears and killing and cooking their own food at ages four and five—without any adult supervision! I began to wonder, are we raising inept children here in the West? How important is childhood anyway?

Child Health and Development

Childhood is the period of life in which the majority of our growth occurs—on a physical, emotional, and intellectual level. While puberty manifests major developments in children— growth spurts, hormonal changes, and the development of our talents and intellectual prowess in a structured environment—it is the growth that occurs between birth and early childhood that is actually most marked. Consider the fact that an infant is born at around one and a half feet tall and approximately eight pounds in weight, but can be over three feet tall and 40 pounds by age four. That is a doubling of height and 500% increase in weight in only four years, a growth spurt that most people won't match again throughout the rest of their lives! Likewise, a vast majority of our emotional and intellectual growth occurs between birth and the age of seven. Our world views and beliefs about ourselves are largely programmed into us by the time we start school, and the exponential increase in our knowledge base in the years between birth (when we appear vegetable-like but are already wired for potential and profound innate talents) to first grade (by which time we have developed the capacity for language, reading, mathematics, and rudimentary abstract thought) is, again, unmatched throughout the rest of our lifetime.

Because this is such an important period of growth and development—arguably the MOST important period—it is essential that parents facilitate healthy growth, exploration, and learning when their children are young. Proper nutrition, attentive care, an emphasis on the importance of healthy socialization, and the value of learning are essential facets of successful child rearing.

But just as important is the facilitation of healthy, constructive play. When children are in the process of growing and discovering the world, the tool that they use for learning is play. Thus, the play that we allow, encourage, and facilitate will have a direct effect on their physical, emotional, and intellectual development. By facilitating child-led play that requires imagination and inventiveness—rather than the structured, marketed, often digitally driven play that has come to dominate our society—we can give our kids a huge advantage when it comes to their early childhood development.

Nyla discovering the joy of using a giant dandelion weed as a crown.

The Backyard Play Revolution

From my experiences over the last six years and the accompanying research I've completed, I've come to understand the value of unstructured play and the opportunity that the backyard presents in our modern day.

Unstructured play is beneficial to my children's health and physical, emotional, intellectual, interpersonal, and spiritual growth. The framework I've found that helps drive unstructured play consists of four core ideas: outdoor play, divergent play, child-led play, and risky play. In order to effectively facilitate unstructured play, Playwork and the role of the adult/parent Playworker provides tremendous guidance.

Loose Parts encourage children's creativity and imagination, and, in many ways, are not always presented as toys at all. Instead, Loose Parts are things children will play with for hours, days, and seasons.

I believe that by adopting these ideas—simple changes to how we view the idea of play, toys, and our home spaces—we can transform the experience of our children and reap immediate and long-term benefits. Because the backyard is privately owned space, it presents an unblocked opportunity to revolutionize your children's experience. This is what I call The Backyard Play Revolution.

I'm not advocating replacing all other play and toys entirely. I've found that adopting these ideas as a practice provides balance between many of the other play types and toys that seem to dominate our modern culture. I don't have to work hard to make sure my daughter has Disney's *Frozen* in her life—it's coming from every direction. She's seen the movie, has the books, has countless plastic figurines, and knows the songs by heart. Yet I have not participated in acquiring a single one of those items.

I'm advocating for these ideas because, without parents' and caretakers' direct influence, children likely will pulled in directions not necessarily of your conscientious making.

Fundamentals

I never imagined that as a parent I would be thinking about how my children played. Play seems like a natural, organic, and intuitive experience for children. Yet so much of their opportunities are governed by parents, from their time to their environment to the direction they are given. Fortunately, most children carry their emotions transparently, and so as I observed my own children I was able to see what play tended to work best for them. I found that their level of happiness, engagement, creativity, and imagination correlated to:

- Whether they were playing inside or outside

- Whether they were playing with convergent or divergent toys

- Whether it was adult-led or child-led play

- Whether it was risky play or constrained

This part of the book looks at each of those aspects. Because risk is such an important matter—we want to protect our children, of course—I spent much time exploring how to ensure my children's safety. Because of this, risky play, categories of risk, safety, and safety with Loose Parts will be explored. Lastly, I found that acknowledging child-led play as an idea wasn't enough for me. I have adopted the ideas of Playwork and being a Playworker, which have offered my children vast and powerful benefits.

Indoor vs. Outdoor Play

In my experience, Loose Parts not only afford a magnificent opportunity for children to flex their imaginations and problem solve with a variety of solutions, but also support sensory and motor development, especially when they are enjoyed in outdoor play. This is important because physical play is one of the core ways to help combat the epidemics of childhood obesity, emotional and psychological disease, and sensory integration challenges facing children today.

Over the past three decades, childhood obesity rates have tripled in the U.S. Today, the country has some of the highest obesity rates in the world—one out of six children is obese, and one out of three children is overweight or obese. In the 1970s, five percent of U.S. children age 2 to 19 were obese. By 2008, that number had increased to nearly 17 percent (Child Obesity, Harvard). Childhood obesity is called "one of the most serious public health challenges of the 21st century" by the World Health Organization.

Similarly, more children are diagnosed and treated for ADHD now than ever before (ADHD Throughout the Years, Centers for Disease Control and Prevention). Likewise, early child educators are noting a dramatic increase in the number of children who are behind in their sensory integration, and you can find a plethora of articles that correlate the loss of play with a rise in sensory development issues.

At the same time, children are spending more and more time in front of screens. "According to the Kaiser Family Foundation, two-thirds of infants and toddlers watch a screen an average of two hours a day; kids under age six watch an average of about two hours of screen media a day, primarily TV and videos or DVDs; kids and teens eight to 18 years spend nearly four hours a day in front of a TV screen and almost two additional hours on the computer (outside of school work) and playing video games. This interferes with physical activity, time outdoors, and social interactions" (The Henry J. Kaiser Family Foundation).

When children are consumed by a passive activity and interacting with a screen, their sensory development is halted. This is problematic because birth to age six is a particularly important time for children's sensory and motor development.

Studies indicate a simple remedy for these ailments is to get children outside and playing actively. The following types of play help children build their senses:

- Manipulating heavy objects—pulling, lifting, pushing, throwing

- Moving one's body in space—jumping, running, stepping

- Feeling and playing with a variety of textures—grasping, sweeping, brushing

- Listening to a diversity of natural sounds

Convergent vs. Divergent Play

As my plunge into research continued, I came across an interesting book penned by a trio of

PhDs: *Einstein Never Used Flashcards: How Our Children Really Learn—and Why They Need to Play More and Memorize Less*. The book presents years of developmental research condensed into a simple message: Learning really happens through play. One of the ideas I found most compelling in the book was the concept of convergent versus divergent play. Convergent play, like convergent problems, has only one solution. The "ability to solve convergent problems has been linked to successful performance on standard classroom and intelligence tests where there is only one right answer." In contrast, divergent play requires a greater amount of imagination, tinkering, and creativity because there is not a single solution. These types of open-ended toys—like Lego blocks, magnetic tiles, and Loose Parts—positively influence children's ability to problem solve, as they require thinking outside of the box.

In my experience, toys that require divergent problem solving and play get far more attention and engagement than toys that have a single fixed solution (with the exception of video games, which seem to be laced with reward and other psychological triggers to generate a form of addiction).

Adult-Led vs. Child-Led Play

Somewhere along the line I stumbled upon the concept of adult-led versus child-led play. In short, there has been a decline in children's opportunities for child-led play, which has been replaced by more structured activities (in part due to the pressure parents feel to play one-on-one with their children). For some time, I struggled with a model or framework for understanding how best to facilitate child-led play myself. Then I came upon the idea of Playwork and the Playworker, which is a nice framework for understanding the role of the adult in child-led play. This is discussed in more detail a bit later.

Loose Parts

Adventure Playgrounds built in the 1970s in Europe originally inspired the concept of—and the name—Loose Parts. Adventure Playgrounds were a response to the shifts in childhood and provided a space and materials that children could interact with, without specific instructions or rules and in a child-led setting. Architect Simon Nicholson was inspired by the materials being used in these adventure parks and the results they were bringing. He coined the term "Loose Parts" and crafted a theory around it. In

How NOT to Cheat Children - The Theory of Loose Parts, Simon states, "In any environment, both the degree of inventiveness and creativity, and the possibility of discovery, are directly proportional to the number and kind of variables in it."

While there appear to be hundreds of Adventure Playgrounds in Europe, there are only a few in the U.S., and this difference is often attributed to liability issues. (National Public Radio covered this years ago in an article titled "Adventure Playgrounds' a Dying Breed in the U.S.") As I learned about these Adventure Playgrounds, I desperately wanted to visit one. But for those of us who don't live close to them, it is possible to introduce Loose Parts to our own backyards and make our own Adventure Playgrounds!

Loose Parts can range from organic materials like tree parts, sand, and rocks to construction materials like buckets, ropes, and boards. They can also include fabric, tires, and just about anything.

Loose Parts are different than traditional toys because they:

- Can be acquired freely or for a fraction of the price of traditional toys

- Profoundly support the developmental needs of the child at a critical age

- Are safer than other toys and play equipment because of how they reduce risk

- Reduce sedentary play, giving children an easy way to be more active

- Are better at fostering imaginative play

- Make spending time outdoors and in nature appealing to children

- Are not marketed as character toys and so do not encourage brand loyalty

- Do not engulf children in a consumer net that drives repeat purchases

When you start to introduce them into your backyard, keep in mind the fundamental principles of Loose Parts.

Fundamentals of Loose Parts:

- They should be novel objects that children gravitate towards naturally. Thus, objects should be added and removed frequently.

- They should be open-ended, with no directions or fixed solutions, and interoperable within the environment and each other, thus presenting infinite play possibilities.

- They should be easily movable by children, so that they can manipulate their play experiences.

Following the guidelines above, you will find that children consistently surprise you with the range and diversity of their imaginations, inventiveness, and innovation in their play. I have found that Loose Parts get more play attention than other man-made toys. In addition, research on early child play has shown that children prefer Loose Parts to manufactured playground equipment and toys.

Finding Loose Parts

A collection of wooden loose parts, sourced from backyard tree cuttings, home improvement stores, and a local sawmill.

Unlike traditional toys, Loose Parts can be acquired freely or inexpensively, and are widely available. Unfortunately, and in part due to how easy it is to find Loose Parts for so little cost, there is not significant support for parents from the various "child-rearing" industries.

However, Loose Parts are actively employed by childhood educators and advocates. Loose Parts are used as part of a core curriculum and/or the play environment. They can be found in a variety of not-for-profit and educational settings, including:

- Reggie Emilia schools, Waldorf schools, and other forward-looking and outdoor-focused schools

- Various playgrounds and public gardens

- Hundreds of public playgrounds—Adventure Playgrounds—across Europe, and the few in the U.S.

- Parents and caretakers working to incorporate Loose Parts into their backyards

My journey into Loose Parts started with great hesitation. It was hard to believe that my children would prefer Loose Parts to more traditional toys. Traditional toys have beautiful packaging, a story that is emotionally appealing, a bulleted list of benefits my children will receive, and the presence of a price tag, all of which make me think I'm getting something of value.

Because of the lack of widely available information about Loose Parts, I remained cautious and mostly experimented with Loose Parts that I could find for free. When my father cut down a tree in his yard, I gladly brought home a few stumps for my children's play. After trimming our apple tree, I went about cutting small coins from the branches for their play. I found that my garage was full of unused home building materials, wood, canvas, paintbrushes and poles, buckets, and the sorts of things that children could be given and enjoy. Of course, there are other options for how to obtain Loose Parts.

How you can find Loose Parts for free:

- Find unused things at home.
- Let friends know you are looking.
- Keep a lookout for free things left on the curb.
- Watch the free listings on Craigslist.com.
- Contact nearby services that collect organic materials and building materials for disposal.
- Contact local retail service businesses that may recycle materials and are happy to donate to your cause.
- Contact schools.

How you can find Loose Parts inexpensively:

- Visit garage sales frequently.

- Buy new materials from stores, including landscaping and home improvement stores.

- Shop online, especially at places like eBay, Etsy, and classified sites like Craigslist.

In the second section of this book I go through the successes that I've seen firsthand experimenting with Loose Parts, as well as examples of Loose Parts that I've seen others use with similar success.

Junk Playground

As I grew convinced of the value of Loose Parts, I decided to stop dipping my toe into the water and instead cannonball straight in. Instead of allowing serendipity to guide the introduction of Loose Parts into my backyard, I actively began researching them.

My journey quickly led me to Adventure Playgrounds, and the mother of all Adventure Playgrounds, the Junk Playground.

Junk Playgrounds were invented through the observation of a Danish landscape architect, C. Th. Sørensen, who found that children did not play in the playgrounds he built. Instead, children played everywhere else, in spaces that gave them the opportunity to control and manipulate their environments, to dream and imagine and create. For those living in the mountains, country, or more rural settings, this is likely how your children already play. Sørensen wondered if children in the city could be given the same opportunity, and so instead of filling a playground with convergent, closed-ended, fixed structures and playthings, a playground was filled with junk. The first of these Junk Playgrounds opened in 1943, in Emdrup, Denmark, with much success.

Three years later, in 1946, Lady Allen of Hurtwood happened to visit the Junk Playground in Emdrup and was greatly inspired. She brought the idea to London and expanded their prevalence greatly, including naming them Adventure Playgrounds. David Ramsey's *Adventure Playgrounds, Playwork, and Loose Parts: A Historical Perspective* is a thorough historical review that is worth a read.

I started collecting examples of these Adventure Playgrounds, and you can check out dozens and dozens of photos of Adventure Playgrounds and

Junk Playgrounds on my Adventure Playgrounds Pinterest board.

The pictures and videos of children playing at Adventure Playgrounds are astonishing. The children have a level of freedom in their play that is unparalleled in other playgrounds. Check out the trailer for *The Land*, a documentary film about the nature of play, risk, and hazard set in The Land, a Welsh Adventure Playground, which illustrates this point beautifully.

The Land. Photograph courtesy of Erin Davis
TheLandDocumentary.com.

The Land. Photograph courtesy of Erin Davis
TheLandDocumentary.com.

Kids run, jump, and swing—not from a "safe" contraption, but from towering heights across rivers and onto unimaginable piles of junk. They build, they paint, they create. They play with fire and sharp tools. It was unlike anything I had come across, and totally changed my view on how children should be playing.

Yet my heart skipped a beat when I saw children running across narrow boards suspended high above the ground, or when I read of children bouncing on trampolines above concrete surfaces and lighting matches to cook in a snow-covered landscape.

Who was keeping the children safe, and how? This burning question led me to the theory and practice of Playwork and Playworkers, which had humble beginnings but is now a full-fledged professional discipline that you can get a degree and build a career in. Playwork, which I also go into in more detail later, provides an awesome and concise framework that gives parents, grandparents, and other caretakers a very specific and effective way to provide supervision and support of children's play.

At the conclusion of this journey, what I really wanted was to take my children—or better, to let my children walk or ride on their own volition—to a neighborhood Adventure Playground. Even though the city I live in has just over 100,000 people, it is no longer rural, and my children are subjected to similar challenges that other children face in large cities. An Adventure Playground would give them such an amazing opportunity. They would enjoy child-led play with Loose Parts. Alas, I searched and found less than half a dozen Adventure Playgrounds in the U.S., and none anywhere near my house.

And so I decided to do it in my own backyard.

Backyard Playspace Opportunity

Nyla studying the beauty of a grasshopper found in the backyard.

Across the literature for early childhood development, much attention has been given to the changes in how parents raise their children. Parents consistently share memories of how they had independence to range far from their homes when growing up, unsupervised by adults. Children were told to "go outside and play" in previous generations, and there they would find many other children doing the same. This gave them access and freedom to interact and play.

My favorite story that demonstrates how dramatically childhood independence has changed is about the Thomas family in Sheffield, England. This story, captured in an article from *Daily Mail*—How children lost the right to roam in four generations—is about how children's independence in where they played dramatically shifted over time:

- Great-grandfather George (age 8 in 1919) was allowed to walk six miles on his own to go fishing.

- Grandfather Jack (age 8 in 1950) was allowed to walk one mile on his own to the woods.

- Mother Vicky (age 8 in 1979) was allowed to walk ½ mile on her own to go to the swimming pool.

- Son Ed (age 8 in in 2007) was allowed to walk 300 yards to the end of the block.

Similarly, in the USA, the area where children are allowed to roam independently without adult supervision has declined by 90% since the 1970s (Urban Children's Access to Their Neighborhood: Changes Over Three Generations, Sanford Gaster).

There seems to be a multitude of reasons for the dramatic shift. Some of these include:

- Dual-parent working families and single-parent families that require children to be put into structured day care programs.

- Larger homes, more homes, HOAs, and generally denser populations creating less publicly available outdoor space to roam.

- Heightened media attention to the dangers of children playing outdoors without adult supervision—whether real or unsubstantiated—causing parents to fear allowing their children this independence.

- A greater emphasis on the need for children to begin academic preparation to ensure later success as adults, causing parents to put children into programs that promise to educate them.

- Products and programs geared to improving children's physical and developmental capabilities, such as electronic toys, sports, and arts programs, causing parents to schedule structured activities.

A deep look at these issues can be found in *The Atlantic*'s The Overprotected Kid by Hanna Rosin.

While much of the research shows that many of the reasons for reducing children's playtime outdoors are unsubstantiated, the fact remains that children do not range far from their homes. Thus, backyards present one of the most attainable areas for children to play outside. It is a privately owned space, allowing an opportunity that is unblocked for parents to immediately take action.

Risk

Junk Playgrounds raised many questions in my mind about safety. Where do I draw the line? Ropes may not be safe for children to play with unsupervised—as they experiment, they might end up tying themselves inappropriately, and that could lead to bad things. And what about other things like construction materials? But when I introduced one of my old truck tires into the backyard, I saw what happened when the children were left to their own devices.

Articles like the *New York Times*' "Can a Playground Be Too Safe?" and academic works with ridiculously long but apt names such as *Coordinating the Elusive Playground Triad: Managing Children's Risk-Taking Behavior, (While) Facilitating Optimal Challenge Opportunities, (within) a Safe Environment* (Tom Jambor, 1995), quickly made it onto my evening reading list. I became overwhelmed with information about how the current play opportunities for my children in public spaces were riddled with poor design. I started to turn back to history to better understand how we got to where we are today.

In the book *Kith: The Riddle of the Childscape* (the book I recommend you read next!), Jay Griffiths shares stories of children's behavior across cultures. Some of these include:

- Once out of infancy, Native American children were traditionally free to wander wherever they wanted, through woods and water.

- Ache boys of Paraguay are given bows and arrows when they are around two.

- Alacaluf children of Patagonia use shellfish spears and cook their own food at age four.

- In the Amazon, five-year-olds wield machetes.

- By about the age of seven, Inuit boys handle knives, become familiar with rifles and trap lines, and from then on "travel with the men, as hardy a traveller as any of them."

- In Igloolik in the Arctic, eight-year-olds use Inuit knives to carve up frozen caribou without accidents.

These stories expanded my understanding of what children are capable of (although many of the experiences listed here were based on children living in indigenous cultures where there are models, support, and necessity driving behavior), and gave me motivation to keep searching for modern day guidelines.

Categories of Risky Play

In hopes of finding a baseline for children growing up in a modern European, American, or Canadian culture, I came across numerous studies completed over a number of years identifying and confirming types of risk-taking in children's play.

The six categories of risk-taking or risky play include:

1. Play with great heights and danger of injury from falling

2. Play with high or uncontrolled speed and pace that can lead to collision with something or someone

3. Play with dangerous tools that can lead to injuries

4. Play near dangerous elements where children can fall into or from something

5. Rough-and-tumble play where the children can harm each other

6. Play where the children can disappear or get lost

Understanding these behaviors gave me a good sense of a baseline for how children inherently want to play as they work to develop their motor functions and other senses. But is it safe? Or is it safer to keep them on the couch sedated with electronics, rather than allowing them to take risks that make one's heart jump?

Loose Parts Safety

The studies I've reviewed present compelling evidence of the value of risky play, and that play areas comprised of Loose Parts pose fewer hazards for children and result in fewer major injuries (those that require emergency room visits) than traditional playgrounds.

A nice summation of safety concerns and Loose Parts can be found in *Why Children Play Under the Bushes,* by Ruth Wilson, Ph.D. And a more in-depth look at risky play can be found in the 2015 paper *What is the Relationship between Risky Outdoor Play and Health in Children? A Systematic Review* published by the *International Journal of Environmental Research and Public Health.*

While it seems counterintuitive that risky play with Loose Parts has a higher level of safety than other play types, consider that:

- Loose Parts provide high play affordability. As children are able to manipulate materials and their environment, their level of engagement is higher, and correspondingly their level of boredom is lower. This results in lower risk-taking behavior and fewer major injuries.

- Loose Parts tend to be close to the ground, whereas traditional playground equipment (swing sets, playhouses, monkey bars, etc.) tends to be higher off the ground. While children might be falling more, they fall from a lower heights and thus the damages are far less severe.

- Loose Parts play frequently emerges on a small scale, where children are examining and exploring novel materials that they manipulate with their bodies within small spaces (like "painting" the tire with water). On the other hand, traditional playgrounds present greater hazards and result in more emergency room visits. (See above *Why Children Play Under the Bushes.*)

- Loose Parts are, by their very nature, loose and unconnected, such that contact with the material results in less of an impact. In contrast, traditional playground equipment and outdoor toys are frequently fixed and secured in the ground, such that contact with wood, hard plastic, or metal is more like contacting a wall or hard surface.

Personal Safety Practices

In all of my experiences with Loose Parts in the backyard, the children have never been badly hurt. The materials we're playing with do tend to be heavy and the children do tend to manipulate them—stacking, jumping, and hanging—but beyond scrapes and bruises, there have been very few negative results. That being said, the experiences have not been without much fear and anxiety on my part.

There are a variety of steps that I have taken that you can follow to ensure your Loose Parts are as safe as possible:

- Avoid introducing objects that have sharp edges.

- Avoid introducing objects that have nails or other protruding objects that children might not see when playing.

- For organic materials such as tree parts, remove knobs, protruding pieces, and sharp ends. I often will lightly sand organic materials to reduce splinters.

- Don't "help" the children build contraptions or lift them. By avoiding helping children, you will help ensure that they are only able to manipulate objects into positions they can easily recover from. This is especially important with younger children who may be attracted to something that is adult-scale, which could present a larger object falling upon them.

- Don't "help" the children climb, jump, or balance on objects. As mentioned above, if you can resist assisting the children, it will make their experience safer, as well as give them the opportunity to face challenges that are appropriate to their abilities.

Following these simple guidelines has helped us avoid severe injuries.

In my quest, I yearned for guidelines on how to parent—and that was how I discovered the idea of Playwork, which has illuminated my way and enhanced my approach to fostering play with my children.

Playwork and Being a Playworker

Silas examining a tree part placed in the backyard, but with no instruction given.

If children came with manuals, instructions on how to be an effective Playworker would have to be included. Playwork is a powerful idea that has served me well in supporting my children's play and the toys they use.

The origin of Playwork can be traced back to the early Adventure Playgrounds that were staffed by "wardens." But the wardens were not educators or therapists trying to engage children in a specific agenda. Rather, they began as traditional wardens whose responsibilities focused on holding the keys for sheds that held tools, building materials, and other items the children needed for play. Over time, the Playworker's role evolved (as well as their name), and today Playwork is a recognized and respected profession built on a foundation of theory and practice.

The most immediate way to grasp how Playworkers view their role is through a definition of play:

"Play is a set of behaviors that are freely chosen, personally directed, and intrinsically motivated" (Penny Wilson, *The Playwork Primer*, Alliance for Childhood, 2009).

The Playworker's role, then, is to support and facilitate play, rather than trying to educate, train, or treat children through any set of rules, games, activities, or other agendas.

"It is the job of a Playworker to ensure that the broadest possible range of play types can be engaged" (as quoted by Wikipedia from Bob Hughes 2006 book *Play Types: speculations and possibilities*).

When I first learned about Playwork, it resonated deeply with me, and echoed the sentiments I was feeling in observing and playing with my children. As a Playworker, the job of the parent isn't to make sure the child is having a good time, or to direct them in any way. The Playworker is more focused on making sure the children have what they need for their play—such as materials, tools, time, and space.

Playworker job duties:

- Create and maintain a safe play environment.

- Develop a space filled with prompts for exploratory, imaginative, and creative play.

- Allow children to follow their own agendas rather than adult urges.

- Observe from a distance, letting children move about physically on their own.

- Act (upon request) as a character in children's role-playing.

- Introduce new ideas through questions or by briefly modeling play behavior.

A wonderful introduction to Playwork is given by Penny Wilson in a book called *The Playwork Primer*. You can find that, along with additional information, at the Alliance for Childhood.

One of the best videos I've found on Playwork is also from Penny Wilson: *Playwork: An Introduction*.

The video is a great place to start. It introduces the responsibility of adults in fostering play and encouraging risk in play, explains how to preserve play, and addresses the role of the Playworker, especially in Adventure Playgrounds. The film features a great collection of images of historical and modern Adventure Playgrounds across the world, and a review of the theory and practice of using Loose Parts. The fundamentals of a Playworker's job are highlighted, such as using observation, reflections, and analysis to better understand children's play, and enhancing the environment holistically for child-play needs.

Play Types

Nyla and Silas enjoying some locomotive play on a series of stumps.

At some point in my research I ran across the 16 play types (as defined by Hughes and found in *The Playwork Primer*). Below is a list of these play types, along with illustrative examples. This deepened my understanding of the range of play types that children can engage with, especially in regard to what toys to provide them with.

1. Symbolic play—when a stick becomes a horse

2. Rough and tumble play—play fighting

3. Socio-dramatic play—social drama

4. Social play—playing with rules and societal structures

5. Creative play—construction and creation

6. Communications play—words, jokes, acting, body and sign languages, facial expressions

7. Dramatic play—performing or playing with situations that are not personal or domestic (e.g., playing "Harry Potter" or doing a "Harry Potter play")

8. Deep play—risky experiences that confront fear

9. Exploratory play—manipulating, experimenting

10. Fantasy play—rearranges the world in the child's fantastical way

11. Imaginative play—pretending

12. Locomotor play—chasing, swinging, climbing, playing with the movements of your body

13. Mastery play—lighting fires, digging holes, games of elemental control

14. Object play—playing with objects and exploring their uses and potential

15. Recapitulative play—carrying forward the evolutionary deeds of becoming a human being (e.g., dressing up with paints and masks, damming streams, growing food)

16. Role play—exploring other ways of being (e.g., pretending to drive a bus, be a policeman, or use a telephone)

The Practice of Mastering

Every child develops at a different pace and has different needs at different times. Loose Parts are particularly good candidates for children's play—they are developmentally inclusive because they are open-ended and can be used by children as they wish.

In children under the age of six, the primary play modality is mastering and innovation. Mastering means that a child will repeat an action or a play experience over and over, dozens of times, until they master it. For example, tying knots with ropes gave my children the ability to master the skill of manipulating heavy line, as well as developing the muscles in their hands and their hand-eye coordination. This was repeated dozens of times, and while the knots were not Boy Scout grade, they would make any Aspiring Good Dad proud that the knot could hold a bucketful of wood. Innovation means that, once a child masters an action, they will then push the boundaries of their new learning. With the example above, once the knots were mastered on low-hanging objects like tree branches, the children moved to the swing set, where they tried their hand at tying the buckets to the high monkey bars.

How to identify mastering and innovation objects:

- Watch what objects the children are drawn to.

- Watch what objects get extra attention from the children.

- Watch what objects the children return to on subsequent play experiences/days.

- Watch what actions the children repeat with the same objects.

Once you identify mastering and innovation objects, look for opportunities to introduce similar objects. For example, if you find the children using string to tie to branches, then introduce rope. If you find the children tying ropes to small buckets, look to introduce larger buckets.

Practice

The combination of my research, understanding the historical context of children's play and playgrounds, and learning the capacity of young children and how they want to play led me to experiment with dozens of Loose Parts in the backyard. Below, I share seven examples, each with a brief narrative of our experience, how you can use the Loose Parts, where you can get them, and alternative materials. Afterwards, I share a list of many more examples of Loose Parts that you can experiment with in your own backyard. While these seven examples may seem simple on the surface, the experiences I've observed my children having with them are quite profound.

#1 Stick

It's late afternoon. The rain clouds have cleared and the sun is shining brightly. I'm high up on our ladder, tending to our one apple tree in our "orchard." The tree is overgrown, dense, jungly. It hasn't been cared for in years. Silas has woken up from his nap, and both he and Nyla watch in wonder as giant branches shimmering with moisture careen down from the sky and ricochet off lower branches like silvery pinball balls. The children "ooh" and "ahh" at every bump and twist. Being an Aspiring Good Father, I decide to give them jobs. I come down from the ladder and set down the tree trimmer. I instruct them to help me clear the branches away from the base of the tree in the orchard and move them to the center of our backyard. I tell them that, once they get all the branches piled up and I finish the trimming, we can all cut them up to be hauled away for compost. Before I finish, they have already given a nod of compliance and race into action. They love trees, leaves, and playing in the fresh air. Nyla grabs a branch and starts to pull it to the center of the backyard. Silas follows. So I pick up the tree trimmer and climb back up the ladder.

The tree is so full that I get lost in the canopy and focus on my work. Every now and then I look down to the base of the tree below and see the children clearing the branches. They aren't fighting over expensive, breakable, manufactured toys or making a mess like they might indoors. I smile. I love when an impromptu plan goes well.

A few minutes later, I hear Nyla tell Silas, "Come in through the door."

The "door??" I turn around on the ladder and peer through an opening in the canopy. I see the massive swath of branches they've been clearing. Instead of a giant pile in the center of the yard (as I instructed), they have arranged the branches into a sort of circle, with an open area on the northern side. I see Silas run in through the "door," squealing with glee as he joins Nyla in the space they have apparently dedicated as their "home." Over the next hour, the children scour the yard for containers, sand toys, pebbles, leaves, and other organic materials. A neighbor friend drops by and the three children sit in their new home and begin to sort their materials. When I finish putting the tree trimmer and ladder back into the garage and return, they invite me into their creation. The home has magically morphed into a shop. They introduce me to their collection of products and demand I make payment. I find some nearby dandelions that seem to be accepted as tender.

Nyla and Silas surrounded by apple tree branches in their new home.

Rather than removing the branches that day, we decide to leave them in the yard for the children. Because I had cut so much of the tree, the pile of branches was quite large—a good 10' x 8' footprint. It looks like a mess, a tangle, a slash pile, a total blight on our manicured yard. My wife wonders, "When are you going to finish out there"? But for the children, it becomes the basis for imaginative play.

A week later, the children's fondness for the apple tree branches wanes. I cut up the small branches for compost and clean up the larger ones to be used as poles for some unknown future project.

Uses

I've found sticks to be one of the most versatile natural toys in existence. They are a quintessential Loose Part, interoperable and able to be combined with a dizzying array of other toys and scenarios. Some examples include:

- Walls, roofs, floors, windows, and doors for forts, castles, or dens

- Weapons, from swashbuckling swords to pirate pistols

- Mythical, magical, or practical equipment, from wizard staffs to fairy wands to land surveying tools

- A crutch for the wounded or walking stick for the explorer

- Sporting accouterments, from ball field goals to obstacle course materials

- Body parts for snowman, stir rods, and straws for potions and concoctions

Where to Get

Wherever trees grow—which is almost everywhere—you can find sticks. If your yard is devoid of appropriate sticks (for example, twigs will not do!) or if you don't have a yard, there are still a lot of good options, including:

- Trees from a friend's land
- Forest Service or yard waste collection sites
- Tree care service providers
- Saw mills and lumber yards
- Online ecommerce stores such as Etsy

I've found that you can get sticks and tree parts for free or close to free from all but online ecommerce stores. Sticks are unique in that they have minimal value commercially. In fact, they are typically costly to dispose of, and people are eager to give them to children. All it takes is a phone call and a short explanation.

Alternative Materials

Consider the range of a stick: full trees and large branches provide poles, and cuts of different lengths provide stumps or slices; there are tree boughs, seeds (depending on the tree), needles, and pine cones; and cutting smaller branches can provide blocks and coins. These expand and enrich the play possibilities, enhancing the profile of an ordinary stick and turning it into a shinning example of a Loose Part.

When sticks from trees aren't available, there are many other good options, including:

- Household rods
- Landscaping materials like bamboo
- Plumbing pipe
- Construction lumber
- Cut-up cardboard boxes
- Closet rods
- Handrail stock from lumbar yards

Alternate materials can be purchased at common home and building stores, like Bed Bath & Beyond and Home Depot. Whenever I buy paint at Home Depot I make sure to get paint stirring rods, as they can be recycled after use into terrifically sized daggers and swords (for those with children inclined towards noble swashbuckling and knight play).

#2 Rope

Nyla sits on the couch. A wickedly joyful smile peers out through the early dawn light cascading over her locks of hair and face. It's her birthday and we're opening presents. The next one is from me. I'm anxious, wondering if she will be confused or disappointed by my gift. She sets her freshly opened shimmering gold princess dress down, brushes aside the dolls, and reaches for the box I wrapped late last night. She feels the weight and shakes it. The irregular balance and sound doesn't trigger any memories. She is perplexed. Her smile fades into curiosity. She pushes onward and tears off the paper. Silas reaches across the couch to assist. The lid is pried open. I almost hold my breath—she's turning six and the last thing we want is a downpour of tears on her special day. She reaches in and slowly, bit by bit, yanks out a rope and pulley. She shrieks with joy. Literally shrieks. I'm so relieved! She "gets it" with such immediacy that a wave of pride charges through my body—I see that I've managed to raise a child who sees a rope and pulley for it's potential: an open-ended, imaginative, creative play opportunity.

Later she instructs me to secure the pulley to a high branch of the poplar tree that flanks our backyard. Nyla quickly retrieves a galvanized steel bucket and ties the end of the bucket to the rope. She and Silas take turns standing and sitting in the bucket as we pull it up. Quickly, another idea strikes them, and we untie the rope and move to the orchard. She asks me to tie the rope to the maple tree and a nearby aspen tree.

It begins to rain, and it's time for Silas to nap. He heads into the house, looking back longingly as Nyla ties the pulley with the galvanized bucket dangling from it to the rope that spans the two trees. Nyla races to the house and returns with rain jackets. She drags the bucket up the line and climbs up the wall by the maple tree, then jumps into the bucket and launches off the wall. The knot she's tied is junk, so the rope slips apart and she tumbles down to the flat landing, crumpling with the bucket. She's bruised—and a bit upset. But her courage does not yet depart her, and she continues the experiments—through the rain, on her birthday, getting soaked with mud and decorated with scratches and bruises.

Nyla pulling a galvanized bucket through the rain, draped from a pulley and a rope tied between two trees. Purpose: play.

Uses

Ropes are special. They can be used independently, but have the added advantage of being able to be connected to just about anything. For this reason, they are joiners. They provide a surprisingly diverse range of play opportunities, whether being used to lift, pull, tie, or swing. Some examples include:

- Create rides, from swings to tight wires.

- Hang buckets that hold water, treasures, or other organic material.

- Secure textile to form forts or castles.

- Create borders to indicate imaginary buildings or obstacle courses.

- "Sewing," such as making capes or secure dress-up clothes.

- Fashion lassos or bridles to play cowboys of the old west.

- Building animal, insect, and mythical creature dens, such as spider webs.

- Tying to trees to create ladders.

- Drawing wild and fantasy beings, like snakes and serpents.

Where to Get

There are a wide variety of different types of ropes, and it can quickly become overwhelming to decide what kind of rope to get. My considerations for a rope included:

- Durability: I wanted a rope that could be left outside and withstand the elements (rain, snow, sun).

- Price: I didn't know if the children would play with the rope, so I was eager to find an inexpensive option.

- Comfort: I wanted something that would feel good in their hands so they would be eager to handle the rope and not be turned off by the texture.

In looking at the different materials that are used to make ropes, some are obviously better when it comes to being left outside in the elements. For example, nylon is a plastic that is far more mildew resistant than a cotton rope. This is one area where I decided to make a trade-off. To keep the price low and find a comfortable rope, I decided to be open to getting ropes that might only make it through one season. You can spend more or sacrifice comfort to get one that will last longer, but I don't think it is worth it.

I began my search by looking for climbing ropes, because I imagined my children wanting a rope strong enough to lift, pull, and hang. Plus, they are colorful and designed for handling with bare hands. However, because climbing ropes are built to hold weight and have all these amazing characteristics of stretch, they cost more. Finding an inexpensive rope really limits your options, which is ok and makes the decision easier.

In our front yard we have a rope swing that is a 1" natural fiber rope tied to a log. This rope is aesthetically pleasing—it has a bit of an iconic/quintessential look to it—and it has lasted for a couple years. But it's very uncomfortable on children's hands and legs, and in retrospect I think they would be happier with a different material. I've tested out some cotton ropes, but those mildew very quickly. If you live in a dryer area, they might work fine.

Notice that strength isn't one of my major considerations. Since the rope was going to be used as a joiner (versus a piece of a tree house, for instance), I figured a rope that can hold hundreds of pounds was no safer than one that would break at 10 pounds—and in fact was perhaps more dangerous.

Once you decide what kind of rope will work best for you, you have a few options of where to get them:

- Climbing gyms (they retire ropes early out of concerns for safety, and either donate or recycle them)
- Sporting good shops or hardware shops
- Specialty shops

Alternative Materials

Two other materials you can use as joiners are:

- Bicycle tubes (with the air valves cut out)
- Chains (with any sharpness removed)

I love using bicycle tubes because bike shops that have service centers replace a lot of tubes that have holes in them. They tend to collect them and then recycle them, and I've found that they are all willing to give you the tubes for free. Use a scissors or Exacto knife to remove the valves. Bicycle tubes are interesting to play with because they are very elastic and create new modes of playing.

Considerations for Pulleys

It's worth getting a pulley or two if you're going to get a rope—they introduce a surprisingly engaging group of physics and mechanics. Children instinctively seem to know how to use pulleys, which might seem counter-intuitive to us as adults. Knowing what kind of pulley to get was not so instinctive.

Here's what I based my decision on:

- Lifting ratio power: I did not want a block and tackle style that could offer something in the 7:1 or more lifting ratio power. This would make it easy for children to lift very heavy things, which, while fun, would require constant adult supervision and did not seem safe. Instead, I wanted a simple pulley that had just one wheel and would limit the amount of lifting power the children could have, equal to their strength.

- Fit: The pulley has to fit the rope.

- Durability: I wanted a metal pulley that wouldn't be easily broken by misuse. I assumed the children would not be pulling evenly, but instead would be putting erratic pressure on the pulley from incorrect angles, etc.

Gift Wrapping Guide

Here's a slight digression that I think is worthwhile mentioning.

I think these toys can be wrapped when given to children. Gift-wrapping is a ceremonial act that indicates the value that you as the gift giver assign to the gift. While it may seem silly to wrap some of these toys, my experience has been that children respond well to receiving a gift when it follows the common patterns of other gifts they receive. That tells them the gift has meaning and that you as the parent see value in the object. The object may not have cost you anything, and it may be used, but wrap it anyway! For large gifts, you can wrap them as you might a bike or other too-big item: Put a bow on them.

Nyla opening her rope and pulley, wrapped for her birthday along with bamboo poles.

Keep in mind that for children who are inexperienced with Loose Parts or other toys that come with no instructions, pictures, or marketing pizzazz, you may need to help them move into action. For these reasons, I tend to:

- Have little to no expectations of how my kids will respond to the toys.

- Start small and inexpensive—ideally free.

- Iterate: if at first you don't succeed then try, try again!

- Don't be afraid of failure (I've had a lot of failures, but I just remove them).

- Expect internal and inter-family conflicts about some items that may blemish the backyard.

#3 Tire

It is 2:30 PM and Silas is napping. I put the lawnmower and weed whacker back into the garage and return to the backyard. There are gardening and weeding tools scattered around. I walk around admiring how nice our backyard looks after having spent the morning cleaning it up. The trees are in full leaf, delicately slicing streams of sunshine across the grass. A robin soars from one bough across to a post on the fence that runs along the side of the yard, then drops down to pluck up some twigs and flutters away. Squirrels hop along the base of the apple tree in the orchard. I can hear gurgles from the stream in the valley beyond our gates. It's pretty idyllic. Then I remember I need to get my car tires replaced. I wonder if my children would enjoy playing with one of the car tires.

An hour later, I've returned from the local tire shop. I learned that the tire shop charges a fee to recycle tires when you purchase new ones. Instead of paying the fee for each of the four tires, I decide to keep two of them. We wash the tires off in the driveway. With a slight bit of trepidation and anxiety, I roll one of the used tires into the beautifully appointed backyard. Silas is awake now and the children have been watching as I put a piece of my vehicle in the backyard. I step back, hoping for the best...

In no time, the children have climbed aboard the tire, as it lies on its side. They circle about the rim, balancing by holding each other's hands, laughing and crashing and climbing aboard over and again. They find a nearby watering can, fill it to the brim, and return to "paint" the tire with water. At one point—and with much tenacity— the children lift the tire upright. They proceed to try to balance on it, but fail, bombing down into the freshly cut blades of grass. Then Nyla climbs into the tire, her body performing a contortion to weld her shoulders and limbs into the recesses of the rubber. The instant her last limb is brought into the cavity, the balance is compromised and the tire teeters, with her in it, landing flat against the ground. I imagine the weight of an asphalt-grade vehicle part crushing down upon her small figure. My heart skips a beat. She is facedown inside the tire and not making a sound. I run towards them with the vision of her emerging with a bloody mangled face racing through my mind. But as I near the tire, she untangles her pretzel self and emerges, with scrapes and a burst of glee dancing across her face.

Nyla and Silas getting acquainted with the car tire newly set in our backyard.

Later, the sun cuts past the tree boughs and heats up the lawn. They children have managed to move one of the baby pools next to the tire. They've filled the pool with a few inches of water and are jumping from the tire into the pool. It is a slippery proposition. They slide and fall and crash more, cooling off from the heat.

Of course, having a used automobile tire in the backyard draws criticism from my wife. When she comes out to inspect the goings-on—with an iced drink and her sun hat, having just showered off the day of gardening to enjoy the beauty we'd created—her face gives way to a quiver of sadness when she sees the car tire smack dab in the middle of the lawn. Moments later, however, her mood brightens when she sees how much fun the children are having.

Her reaction was exactly what I was feeling as I had rolled the tire around back. Is this crazy? Am I making our backyard look like a...a junkyard? Eventually, I rolled the tire into the sandbox, where it is less of a visual atrocity but still easily accessible.

Uses

The rubber that tires are made of is resilient and does not attract cats, dogs, rodents, or insects. It also retards weed growth (not to mention grass growth!). Unlike typical wood or fibers, the rubber does not decay (at least at any noticeable rate) since rainy weather and freezing temperatures don't cause it to rot. The Consumer Products Safety Committee reports that tires used in playgrounds do not catch fire, do not leach, are not toxic, and have a documented cushioning benefit. If tires are treated with paint, flammability concerns are even further reduced. These characteristics provide a long life for a tire in a playspace. Their shape and buoyancy lend them to some lovely play opportunities, including:

- Climbing, jumping, and building (such as jungle gyms or structure building)

- Lifting and rolling (creating an unusually large but light toy for circus and sporting-type games)

- An instant space for crawling and residing, such as forts, dens, and launch pads

- Planter box, such as growing flowers and other flora

Where to Get

Buying new tires is not ideal, due to the cost. However, as I discovered, tire service centers face the challenge of what to do with used tires that have been replaced on their customer's vehicles. Thus, they provide an ideal source. But there are other options as well:

- Your own tires after they have been replaced.

- Tire service centers (just call them!).

- Smaller tires can be acquired from places that have go-carts and other amusement park rides that use tires.

- Larger tires can be acquired from working farms after use.

- Automobiles, farm equipment, hardware supply stores (think wheelbarrow wheels).

Tires work best as Loose Parts when they are sized such that the children can manipulate them. Tires too large for small children to move about become less engaging.

Drainage

When designers use tires in playgrounds, they consider drainage. For example, some designers require holes to be drilled in the tires to allow drainage, while others fill the tires with sand to impede water collection. What's unusual about tires is that when the water does collect in the recesses, it is surprisingly difficult to get out due to the lip of the rim. I've found you can't quite get it out just by flipping and dropping the tire about. I used a ¼" drill bit to drill four holes in either side of the rim to ensure water drained and didn't accumulate and get yucky.

Alternative Materials

- Gymnastic landing mats, ramps
- Inflatable swimming tires
- Reclaimed industrial wooden spools (also known as wire or cable reels)

These types of materials can be found at Etsy, Amazon, or Home Depot stores.

#4 Bucket

It's early morning and we've returned from a short bike ride around nearby Wonderland Lake. Lunch is a ways away, so I decide to make a run for some supplies for the backyard. I load Silas and Nyla up in the car and we drive to a local indoor climbing gym and ask if they have any rope they can donate to our cause. This gym, like others, has an ongoing supply of used climbing ropes that are no longer suitable for climbing. They are a big climbing gym and have a lot of this used rope sitting around, so they are happy to donate some to us as long as we promise not to use it for climbing. We follow the manager into the gym, past multi-story climbing walls studded with holds, and into the back where they store equipment. She pulls out two 50' ropes and four 10' ropes. We are thrilled to get so much rope for free to add to our collection!

It's afternoon now and the cousins have arrived from California for a visit! The children are in the backyard experimenting with the ropes, tying them in spider-web-like configurations, using tree branches, the fence, and—amazingly, finally!—the geodesic dome. Then two medium-sized galvanized buckets draw their attention. Inside of the buckets are dozens of tree coins, thin slices of an aspen tree branch I had made days earlier. They untie a shorter rope from the spider web and secure one end to the handle of the galvanized buckets, then repeat the process with a second bucket. Then they drape the ropes over their shoulders and march to the swing set. The older children climb up the swing set and manage to climb on top of the monkey bars—all while holding the galvanized buckets from the ropes slung over their shoulders. Now the buckets swing down below, where the younger children proceed to remove and replace the tree coins. The buckets are swung back and forth. The children jump. They use all their might to haul the buckets up and down, tying and retying. I wonder what is dancing in their imaginations? Is it a construction site? A sky shop? Are the older children feeding wild animals below with cookies from the clouds? It is anyone's guess, but they are entertained for hours.

Nyla and Silas securing climbing ropes to hang buckets of tree coins.

Uses

Buckets have such incredible capacity for play. For example:

- Carrying supplies
- Mixing potions and soups
- Transporting water
- Building materials for forts and dens
- Use as a ladder
- Use as a swimming hole
- Use as a zip line, or to be hoisted up into the air
- Sand castle building
- Homes for pretend beings

Where to Get

Buckets can be made of just about anything: plastic, metal, wood, glass, and even ceramic. Each material has advantages and disadvantages. Plastic has the advantage of hurting less if the bucket is thrown and contacts a child. Wood has an appealing aesthetic but decays quickest. Glass and ceramic are a nice weight, but can be dangerous if shattered. Metal is a favorite of ours for it's ability to withstand the elements and children's propensity to handle their toys roughly, but can have sharp edges, especially around the handles and lip.

While it is easy enough to find buckets online, I've found that it's nice to see them in person to get a sense of their size. Regardless, you can acquire buckets at some of the following places:

- Landscaping, gardening, farm, and hardware supply stores
- Online at eBay, Amazon, and supply stores

Alternative Materials

You can avoid buying buckets (if you don't have any) by using materials that are typically found in households, including:

- Cardboard boxes
- Discarded pot plant containers
- Kitchen containers (plastic and cardboard milk jugs, for example)
- Cooking pots and pans
- Glasses (I suggest plastic over glass, as glass can easily break)

#5 Sheet

It's a lazy afternoon. Chinook winds kick sand up from the sandbox now and again, dusting the arcs of the children's swinging. They tire of pumping and drift, swing chains clanging haphazardly. The moment slides quietly into entropy. Nearby, rocketing high into the air, is a teepee I made earlier in the day. Or at least part of a teepee. Wielding my Eagle Scout skills, I had lashed four larger tree limbs together in a tripod-like arrangement and then spread each of the legs to create a teepee. I am pleased to see that my skills from decades ago are still intact, but the children are uninterested. As their interest in the swings wanes, I decide to see if I can find a sheet to make the tripod into a more legitimate teepee, with hopes that it will captivate the children. I find a small piece of fabric and return to the backyard.

I wrap the sheet around the legs, rolling it around two of the legs at the ends to create a doorway. It's pretty poorly designed, but is holding its shape. I crawl in. It works! I peak my head out again and yell over to the children, "Come into the teepee!" In a flash they transform into Excitement Rockets, sailing out of the Doldrums and into the Adventure Backyard, diving, sliding, and cascading into the teepee. In no time, they take possession of the teepee and I am given a swift exit. As any new homeowner will, the children quickly begin interior design, furnishing, and slight renovations.

Their favorite toys—from sticks to ropes to buckets—are drawn as if by magnets to this new playspace. The next day and throughout the weeks that follow, the children assume the roles of archaeologists, yet rather than uncovering layers of dirt and time, they rummage through our house in search of sheets. When a suitable sheet is found, it is quickly brought outside and added to the collection of toys and other Loose Parts. The teepee becomes an outpost for a larger village, consisting of sprawling dens constructed at the bases of trees, festival sites on the lawn where colorful mosaics makes up the platform upon which feasts are held, and much more.

Nyla displays her wares beneath the makeshift teepee.

Uses

Sheets are uniquely qualified. They are materials that children can manipulate, but also block out the outside world, making for a private setting beyond the purview of adults (which is important in child development). Because they are flexible and easy to cut and tie, they have a range of other engaging play opportunities. These include:

- Material for floors, walls, ceilings, doors, teepees, forts, dens, and homes

- Slung around the body as robes, capes, dresses, and general ceremonial garb

- Corners pulled together to create a bag for carrying things

- An accessory for built/imagined creatures, or material for building a creature (think dragon, snowman, etc.)

- Decoration of a playspace (think hanging a tapestry in one's home, but outside and by children)

- Roadways in a playland

Where to Get

While sheets can be purchased at obvious bed and bath type stores, these are also a perfect material to find used or recycled. You can find sheets at these types of places:

- Extras in your own house that are too old too use

- Friends who may have extras that are not used

- Online or brick & mortar bed and bath stores

- Garage sales
- Second-hand stores

Alternative Materials

Sheets combine ideal size and softness. However, there are a lot of different types of textiles that work nicely and have other benefits. Some include:

- Towels (especially good for lying on top of grass, and snow play)
- Silks and sarongs (lightweight and small, easy for smaller children to use)
- Canvas (more durable than most sheets, some canvas includes waterproof backing)
- Tarps (come in a variety of sizes, well-suited for a variety of surfaces, waterproof, relatively inexpensive)
- Large pillows (nice for floors, walls, stacking)
- Tapestry, rugs, carpet

#6 Water

"Hey guys, I know! It's perfect!" Nyla says as we drive home after a visit to Home Depot. Being inspired by the last few months of Loose Parts play in the backyard, I have decided to test out some construction materials that I'd seen documented at playgrounds and preschools around the Web: vinyl gutters and PVC pipe. When I first took the materials off the shelf at Home Depot, I felt a wave of anxiety and awkwardness. Was I really buying gutters and pipe for my children to play with as toys? Yes, yes I was. Are they really going to play with them? I don't know. The gutter cost $3.97. Together with the pipe, they cost less than a couple cups of Starbucks coffee. I knew that bringing them home and putting them into the playspace would make the backyard look like a junkyard. This was a fully committed plunge into the world of Loose Parts and Adventure Playgrounds.

But my fears quickly melt away on the drive home. Nyla is excited, and her excitement is contagious.

When we arrive home, I carry the gutter and pipe into the backyard. And then something unexpected and magical happens. The children quickly set to gathering other Loose Parts and begin crafting something spellbinding. They tie the gutter up to a low limb on a tree using rubber bicycle tube. They make an arrangement of miscellaneous boards, buckets, and containers, and place the loose end of the gutter on top of these. They collect tree coins and then run into the house to find an array of discarded bath toys—a dilapidated mermaid and two spare yellow ducks—before returning to their creation.

They move a garden hose to the top of the gutter, securing it with more bicycle tubes, and then turn it on full blast. They have created a water slide! For the next hour they launch tree coins, mermaids, and ducks down the slide. Eventually, the bicycle tube lashing loosens and the slide crashes. They resolve to balance it on the mess of planks and buckets, and continue. At one point, the hose is attached to the end of the PVC pipe, which has been moved to the deck above the backyard. A giant stream of water plumes through and down from the end of the pipe, a cascading waterfall crashing into the gutter. It is magnificent. Games of nonsense ensue, with the children collecting and placing tree coins in elaborate sequences, only to watch them get pushed by waves of water and roll across the slide.

It's time for lunch—and I hear thunder, which means rain. I start picking things up. "Maybe it's just a giant stepping on the ground," says Nyla.

They're glued to it. Minutes later I have to physically remove them from the backyard and into the house for lunch.

Nyla and Silas running tree coins down the water-filled vinyl gutter.

That day, they return to the backyard two more times. Silas is so adamant about wanting to keep playing that he refuses to nap. They negotiate to eat dinner outside, and by bedtime I remove the third set of soggy, muddy, grassy, dirty outfits and put the children down for a well-deserved slumber. Yeehaa!

Uses

Water is magnetic. It draws children in any environment and holds their attention for hours. To allow water into the realm of toys, it is best to find a way to make it self-serve. In my experience, garden hoses are a good start for this, but children will often leave the water running indefinitely. To regulate water use, I've found a simple self-closing sprayer works well. Likewise, I've found self-closing spigot attachments work. Other useful approaches include large containers of water, whether entirely open like a bucket, or five- to seven-gallon water jugs with plastic spigot spouts. My favorite—although more expensive and requiring some assembly—are hand pumps that can be mounted on 30-gallon containers. With self-serve water, so much is possible. Some examples:

- Water slides, whether for children or objects
- Tubs for washing bodies, clothes, parts
- Supply for making soups, potions, and other concoctions, whether as part of an outdoor mud kitchen or independently
- Source for pools, ponds, bird baths
- Rivers and landscaping

- Watering plants, flowers, and other things the children might wish to grow

- Painting on rocks, fences, decks, and other surfaces

- Pouring and practicing other motor skills

Where to Get

Parts to facilitate self-serve water can be found in a variety of places:

- Garden, landscaping, or home improvement supply stores

- Online at Amazon, eBay

- Garage sales, free stuff on curb, or Craigslist

Alternative Materials

If you're not interested in buying or sourcing anything new or used, your own kitchen can surely spare some containers to carry water to the backyard!

7 Mud Kitchen

Saturday morning and my wife is at an exercise class. I decide to stay at home, and have managed to get the children outside by around

9:30 AM. They seem bored, and I'm a bit bored too. I survey the backyard and see one unfinished project after another. There's our neglected land we want to convert into a garden. There's our orchard that was manicured the previous summer but is now in dire need of weeding. There's the row of bushes and trees that all need trimming. Closer to the house along the side fence are unused trellis. I think of all the outdoor kitchens—mud kitchens—that have inspired my wife and me to dream of crafting one of our own. The pictures online present kitchens that are elegantly designed with serious craftsmanship— no doubt the work of Super Dads. I glance back across the lawn and see my children mulling about in the weeds and sandbox. I wonder what can be accomplished in a day, using the spare trellis and other junk that might be piling up in our garage. I head into the garage and see an old IKEA spice rack and hooks. I decide to see what I can fashion quickly that my children can play with that morning.

Just 30 minutes later, I've screwed the trellis to a rotting old plank and attached four 2x4s for legs. Nyla and Silas help me carry the rickety contraption to the backyard and we place it beneath the deck. We forage for some sand, dirt, leaves, twigs, and other organic material. I put some water into a sand bucket and presto—we have a mud kitchen. The children immediately start playing with the mud kitchen and continue to do so for hours.

Nyla and Silas mixing potions in the rickety mud kitchen.

Uses

While mud kitchens have the primary function of providing an outdoor kitchen to "cook" in, they can lead to all sorts of play around the backyard. Some of these include:

- Cooking in the mud kitchen
- Collecting organic materials for the mud kitchen
- Transporting water to the mud kitchen
- Creating a dining room for the "feast"
- "Feasting"
- Setting up drying racks for mud creations

Where to Get

While you can buy elaborate pre-fabricated mud kitchens of excellent craftsmanship, I suggest sourcing materials simply and progressively over time, allowing children to co-create their kitchen.

- Garage sales
- Free stuff left on sidewalks
- Free stuff offered on Craigslist
- Your garage or friends' garages
- Your indoor kitchen

Alternative Materials

- Cardboard boxes
- Crates

I hesitated to include the mud kitchen as one of the toys in this book because of how elaborate it seems. But it has been one of our more outstanding experiments for two years running, and you can actually start very simply—see my book *Mud Kitchen in a Day* for more info.

Ingredients

It's a hot Saturday. We unload from my Land Rover and open the back to view our prize: a straw bale that we picked up from Harlequin Gardens, a nearby nursery and garden center. The children eye the straw bale with amusement and wonder. I lift the straw bale out of the back in a flurry of straw pieces and dust. As the debris settles, I urge the children to grab the baling rope on the far end of the bale. They do, and we awkwardly carry it around the side of the house, through the gate, and into the backyard. We pause for a moment to reorient ourselves. The straw bale juxtaposes our manicured lawn, lending it a farmyard aura. We decide to place the straw bale on the northeast side of the yard, off to the side of the swing set and somewhat obscured by large lilac bushes. There we have a collection of small stumps and a rotted old post that butts up against the fence.

The children get to work immediately and without instruction. Nyla pulls straw out from the bale one stalk at time at first, and then in handfuls. Silas mimics her, and soon they have handfuls of straw. Nyla marches out from the enclosure of stumps and lilacs and walks towards the big tree between the swing set and the house. She arrives at the base and crouches down, then arranges the straw in a roundish-type design and scampers off. Silas does the same. They repeat the process another half dozen times and then scrounge up rocks and other tidbits to place in the center of the round straw pilings. These, they announce, are nests.

I imagine experiences like this are common for those living on farms where straw is plentiful. We live in what's called rural North Boulder, and while some residents keep chickens, goats, and other animals on their property, our small backyard is not filled up with these kinds of things. I am amazed at how quickly the straw bale is accepted and incorporated into the children's play.

Following is a list of Loose Parts that you can introduce into your own backyard.

Nyla manufacturing her own tree coin toys.

Organic

- Bark
- Grass
- Leaves
- Logs
- Mulch
- Pine cones

- Rocks
- Reeds
- Seeds
- Shells
- Stones
- Stumps
- Tree slices (coins, pancakes, etc.)
- Twigs
- Woodchips

These are by far some of my favorites. In some cases, the material is too heavy for children to manipulate by themselves, such as large logs or stumps. I like to think of those as part of the playspace, and welcome habits such as hammering nails into them or crushing rocks into dust (versus trying to protect their pristine, unblemished quality).

Junk/Recycled/Hardware

- Buckets (galvanized/plastic, of varying sizes)
- Cable ties
- Car tires

- Child-size wheelbarrow
- Chains
- Containers
- Cord
- Crates
- Inner tubes of bicycles (cut into lengths with the valves cut out)
- Rope
- Poles
- Pulleys
- String
- Shipping pallets that are heat-treated and stamped with "HT"
- Wagons

Getting anything that has been previously discarded or recycled takes a bit of gumption. It is going to be dirty—you can wash it. It is going to have dents—kids will add to those. You might be dumpster diving—well, not really. Most supplies like these end up as single-stream recyclables, so while you may be retrieving from some sort of disposal bin, you are not going to be dealing with bio-waste.

Textile

- Blankets
- Canvas
- Cushions
- Drop cloths (ground cloth, tarps, etc.)
- Sheets
- Towels

These are all great for making forts, cubbies, or den areas. It is helpful to have a place to store these—ideally inside of the house to keep them easily accessible but out of the elements to minimize deterioration (depending on your location, this may or may not be a problem).

Kitchen

- Bowls (large metal or plastic)
- Canisters
- Condiment containers
- Cooking tins
- Cooking utensils (the sturdier the better!)
- Drainer for dishes
- Pans

- Pots
- Sifter, colander
- Spice shakers
- Towels, dishrags, pot holders

Although Loose Parts have, by definition, no fixed use, these items tend to work really well with other "true" Loose Parts. They may or may not be used in the way you would expect, but are great for stimulating creative, imaginative play scenarios.

Farm Supplies & Equipment

- Hand pump
- Horse shoes
- Hose
- Miscellaneous farm tools
- Straw bale
- Tub

I find these items—with the exception of the hose—harder to come across freely, but they add an intrinsic richness to play when you can obtain them.

Landscaping Materials

- Dirt

- Boulders

- Bricks

- Flagstone of various dimensions and weights

- Glass pebbles

- Mulch (different textures and colors)

- Pavers

- Pea gravel

- River stones (fairly smooth "pebbles" of about four to six inches)

- Sand (colored and plain)

- Sawdust

- Stones (different sizes and colors)

It is worth experimenting with the quantity of landscaping materials. I've found that constraining the quantity of something allows the children to treasure it for its relative uniqueness. For example, sawdust in vast volumes tends to be avoided, while a small handful becomes a prize.

Construction Materials

- 4-8 planks that are springy, maybe 6"
  wide, no knots in wood (get at least 6)

- 6' vinyl gutters x 4

- 10' vinyl gutters x 2

- Galvanized steel garbage cans

- PVC pipe

- Pipe insulation

- 30-gallon plastic tub with top

If you're going to get into these types of
materials—and I strongly recommend that you
do—you will be well served by suspending your
judgment while at the hardware store. I consider
myself pretty open-minded, but I felt like a real
fool spending my weekend morning buying a
piece of vinyl gutter for the kids—until they
started playing with it!

Reflections

Over the last six years I have dramatically changed how I view spending time with my children and what kind of things and experiences to provide for them. Encouraging outdoor, divergent, and risky play, facilitated through the practice of Playwork, has had a profound impact on how my children play, as well as my role in this play. Loose Parts can be recycled, found, or purchased inexpensively, and provide hours, days, weeks, and seasons of engagement. These ideas support healthy child development in an age when our children's activities, interactions, and attention can easily slip into the hands of those who have a focus on growing their own businesses rather than a human.

My experiences in the last six years have transformed how I see raising children and provided a wealth of joy and happiness for our family. I hope this book will help you begin your own journey.

My parting advice is to begin now, today—or tomorrow at the latest! You can revolutionize your children's backyard experience inexpensively—it demands little more than a shift in your perception of your role as a parent and your children's needs in their own journey.

The End

I hope you enjoyed my book. If you learned a few things and found it interesting, I would be very grateful if you would consider leaving a review on Amazon so others might enjoy it, too. Thanks!

Extra Help To Get Started

I've created a Screen-Free Outdoor Play Planner that you can download and print as a worksheet to get started. It includes the Loose Parts List from earlier in the book as a handy reference. It's free on my website. Get the Screen-Free Outdoor Play Planner and Loose Parts List here: http://jasonrunkelsperling.com/screen-free-outdoor-play-planner

About the Author

I spent the early part of my childhood in a mountain community west of Boulder, Colorado. My father built our house and it was a child's dream: permanent toy spaces, indoor climbing, crawlspaces you could sleep in, decks abounding, a bridge to the front door and back door, butted up against a rock outcropping, and topped off with giant vistas of the Rocky Mountains bowing down to the Eastern Plains. We were surrounded by wilderness, where wild things roamed—deer, bear, raccoons, coyote, and more. We were wild children. And so were the neighbors that we could visit without parental supervision at an early age.

Today, I am a husband and father to two young children. I returned to Boulder, Colorado, where I currently reside. I am an Eagle Scout and experienced outdoorsman, have traveled in 5 continents and 45 US states, and have lived in Asia and Australia for 2 years. I have documented my outdoor adventures with my children on TheAdventureDad.com for years, founded the Running Wild Family Nature Club, and spend most of my free time trying to figure out how to increase the time our family spends outside. Professionally, I received my BFA from the University of Colorado before completing an international MBA across three continents. I am currently the director of a software product that helps companies share their messages around the world.

If you have feedback about the book, insight as to how to make it better, or questions you wished were addressed—or just want to get in touch— you can contact me at JasonRunkelSperling.com.

Other Books By Jason

Mud Kitchen in a Day: How to quickly get your kids outside, playing in the dirt, & enjoying creative play.

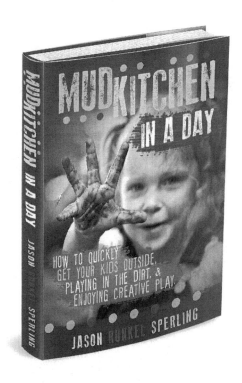

Looking for that perfect summer distraction to get the kids out into the backyard? Learn how to set up a simple and inexpensive children's mud kitchen in a day, allowing your children or grandchildren endless hours of plain and dirty backyard fun. Follow one father's entertaining and informative attempt to get his children outside, offline, and into the mud. Author Jason Sperling takes us inside his experience creating a backyard mud kitchen for his two small children. Full of humor, parenting insight, and in-depth research, Sperling's account will inspire you to create your own mud kitchen in a day, maximizing family fun, bonding, and creativity.

This easy-to-follow guide is appropriate for parents of any skill level and backyards of any size. Forgoing complex design, Sperling's mud kitchen guide focuses on the essential components of a mud kitchen using simple resources, allowing just about anyone to create a stellar children's mud kitchen in only one day.

Dozens of additional resources are included, such as:

- Where to get supplies, whether by making, finding, or buying them

- Outdoor play and its value to child development

- The value of dirt in building strong immune systems

- Comprehensive list of inspiring case studies and photographs of mud kitchens from around the world

Buy *Mud Kitchen in a Day* on Amazon Kindle.

Made in the USA
Middletown, DE
30 January 2016